A Special Gift

For

_____

From

_____

Date

_____

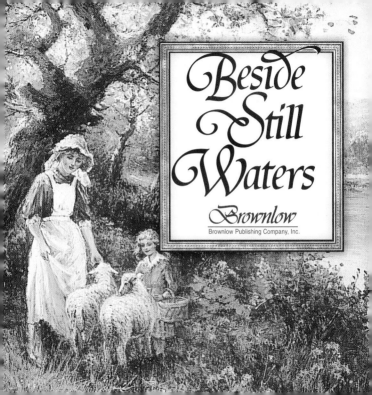

Beside Still Waters

Brownlow

Brownlow Publishing Company, Inc.

Little Treasures
Miniature Books

Faithful Friends

For My Secret Pal

From Friend to Friend

Grandmothers Are for Loving

Mother — The Heart of the Home

My Sister, My Friend

Precious Are the Promises

Quiet Moments of Inspiration

Quilted Hearts

Rose Petals

Soft As the Voice of an Angel

The Night the Angels Sang

'Tis Christmas Once Again

My Shepherd

The Lord is my shepherd;

I shall not want.

He makes me to lie down

in green pastures:

he leads me beside still waters.

∼

PSALM 23:1, 2

$\mathcal{W}$hat different

lives we should lead

if we would

but take things

by the minute.

~

Everlasting Arms

We live today with the everlasting
arms beneath us; we breathe,
we eat, we walk, we think and
dream, all because we are sustained
by a universe greater than ourselves
and preserved by a love
beyond our fathoming.

JOSHUA LIEBMAN

The great soul that sits on the throne of the universe is not, never was, and never will be, in a hurry.

⁓

JOSIAH GILBERT HOLLAND

The world is round and the place which may seem like the end may also be only the beginning.

⁓

IVY BAKER PRIEST

*F*aith is the daring of the soul
to go farther than it can see.

~

WILLIAM NEWTON CLARKE

*E*ternal life does not begin
with death; it begins with faith.

~

SAMUEL SHOEMAKER

$\mathcal{E}$verything true and great grows
in silence. Without silence we fall
short of reality and cannot plumb
the depths of being.

∾

LADISLAUS BOROS

$\mathcal{F}$our things go together:
silence, listening, prayer, truth.

∾

HUBERT VAN ZELLER

When people are serving,
life is no longer meaningless.

JOHN W. GARDNER

Love from one being to another
can only be that two solitudes
come nearer, recognize and
protect and comfort each other.

HAN SUYIN

He Delights to Dwell

All His glory and beauty come from within, and there He delights to dwell. His visits there are frequent, His conversation sweet, His comforts refreshing; and His peace passing all understanding.

~

THOMAS À KEMPIS

Heaven's Glories

No coward soul is mine,

No trembler in the world's

storm-troubled sphere:

I see Heaven's glories shine,

And faith shines equal,

arming me from fear.

EMILY BRONTË

The Peaceable Kingdom

The wolf shall dwell with the lamb,

and the leopard shall lie down with

the kid; and the calf and the young

lion and the yearling together;

and a little child shall lead them.

ISAIAH 11:6

$\mathcal{W}$e never become truly
spiritual by sitting down
and wishing to become so.
You must undertake something
so great that you cannot
accomplish it unaided.

PHILLIPS BROOKS

We must wait for God, long, meekly, in the wind and wet, in the thunder and lightning, in the cold and the dark. Wait, and he will come. He never comes to those who do not wait. He does not go their road. When he comes, go with him, but go slowly, fall a little behind; when he quickens his pace, be sure of it before you quicken yours. But when he slackens, slacken at once; and do not be slow only, but silent, very silent, for he is God.

FREDERICK WILLIAM FABER

The strengthening of faith
comes through staying with it
in the hour of trial.

CATHERINE MARSHALL

Faith is the subtle chain which
binds us to the infinite.

ELIZABETH OAKES SMITH

*W*onder is the basis of worship.

❧

THOMAS CARLYLE

*F*aith builds a bridge from
this world to the next.

❧

ANONYMOUS

*T*hey are well guided that
God guides.

❧

SCOTTISH PROVERB

*The only thing
that makes one place
more attractive to me than
another is the quantity
of heart I find in it.*

~

JANE WELSH CARLYLE

There is nothing
that makes men rich
and strong but that which
they carry inside of them.
Wealth is of the heart,
not of the hand.

JOHN MILTON

A Shepherd's Care

The Lord my pasture
shall prepare,
And feed me with a
shepherd's care;
His presence shall my
wants supply,
And guard me with
a watchful eye.

∽

JOSEPH ADDISON

A Quiet Heart

Humility is perfect quietness of heart.
It is never to be fretted of irritated or
sore or disappointed. It is to expect
nothing, to wonder at nothing that is
done to me. It is to be at rest when
nobody praises me and when I am
blamed or despised. It is to go in and
shut the door and kneel to my
Father in secret, and be at peace.

ANDREW MURRAY

Like a Flock

But he brought his people out
like a flock;
he led them like sheep
through the desert.
He guided them safely,
so they were unafraid.

PSALM 78:52, 53

The capacity to care
gives life its deepest
significance.

PABLO CASALS

*W*here there are sheep,
the wolves are never
very far away.

~

PLAUTUS

*F*ear not, little flock,
for your Father has been pleased
to give you the kingdom.

~

LUKE 12:32

His Kindness Need

God is love, and will not leave you,

When you most his kindness need;

God is true, nor can deceive you,

Though your faith be weak indeed.

SEARLE
MOTHER'S HYMN BOOK, 1836

A Right Heart

Great beauty, great strength,
and great riches are really and
truly of no great use;
a right heart exceeds all.

BENJAMIN FRANKLIN

Only in quiet waters things mirror
themselves undistorted. Only in
a quiet mind is adequate
perception of the world.

HANS MARGOLIUS

Peace within
makes beauty without.

ENGLISH PROVERB

We your people,

the sheep of

your pasture,

will praise you forever.

PSALM 79:13

Let love be purified, and all
the rest will follow. A pure love
is thus, indeed, the panacea
for all the ills of the world.

HENRY DAVID THOREAU

The ways of Providence cannot be reasoned out by the finite mind. I cannot fathom them, yet seeking to know them is the most satisfying thing in all the world.

SELMA OTTILIANA LOVISA LAGERLÖF

Teach us delight in simple things.

RUDYARD KIPLING

He Knows
the Way

Not for one single day
Can I discern my way,
But this I surely know—
Who gives the day,
Will show the way,
So I securely go.

∽

JOHN OXENHAM

Dark as my path may seem to others,
I carry a magic light in my heart. Faith,
the spiritual strong searchlight, illu-
mines the way, and although sinister
doubts lurk in the shadow, I walk
unafraid toward the enchanted wood
where the foliage is always green,
where joy abides, where nightingales
nest and sing, and where life and death
are one in the presence of the Lord.

HELEN ADAMS KELLER

$\mathcal{P}$eace is one of those things, like happiness, which we are sure to miss if we aim at them directly.

～

DOROTHY L. SAYERS

$\mathcal{F}$irst keep the peace within yourself, then you can also bring peace to others.

～

THOMAS À KEMPIS

The wealth of a soul
is measured by how much
it can feel; its poverty
by how little.

❧

WILLIAM ROUNSEVILLE ALGER

Life develops from within.

❧

ELIZABETH BARRETT BROWNING

When we are rightly related to God, life is full of spontaneous joyful uncertainty and expectancy—we do not know what God is going to do next; he packs our life with surprises.

~

OSWALD CHAMBERS

God is our God for ever and ever; he will be our guide even to the end.

~

PSALM 48:14

I Believe

I believe in the sun,

even if it does not shine.

I believe in love, even if I do not feel it.

I believe in God, even if I do not see Him.

~

HANS KUNG

In Childlike Hearts

Thy home is with the humble,

Lord!

The simple are thy blest;

Thy lodging is in childlike hearts;

Thou makest there thy rest.

~

FREDERICK W. FABER

*Faith lifts up
shining arms and points
to a happier world
where our loved ones
await us.*

HELEN KELLER

There can be no unity, no delight of love, no harmony, no good in being, where there is but one. Two at least are needed for oneness.

～

GEORGE MACDONALD

No one can develop fully in this world and find a full life without feeling understood by at least one person.

～

PAUL TOURNIER

Thy Sweet Fold

Father, may we our children lead

In paths of peace to Thy sweet fold;

May ne'er our sin or sad neglect

E'er make them hard,

perverse or cold.

~

God tempers the wind to the shorn lamb.

~

HENRI ESTIENNE

Illustration Credits